Can I Deduct? My Pet.

What Every Business Owner Should Know Before Writing Off Their Pet

By
Cathi Korelin, EA NTPIF, CAA, CTS

This book is intended for educational purposes only and should not be construed as legal or tax advice. Tax laws change frequently. Always consult a qualified Enrolled Agent, CPA, or tax attorney regarding your specific situation.

Dedication

To every loyal dog...

Every hardworking farm cat...

Every horse that helped build a business...

And every entrepreneur who's ever looked at their four-legged friend and wondered,

"I wonder if you're deductible..." This one's for you.

Contents

Introduction

Welcome to the Weirdest Tax Book You'll Ever Read

Let's clear something up right away.

No... Your Labrador isn't deductible because he sleeps under your desk.

Your cat doesn't become an employee because she walks across your keyboard every time you open QuickBooks.

And your goldfish? He's probably the least productive member of the company.

(Although he does attend every meeting.) If you've ever searched Google for:

"Can I deduct my dog?"

You've probably found two kinds of answers.

One says:

"Absolutely! Deduct everything!" The other says: "Absolutely not!"

The truth...lives somewhere in the middle.

As an Enrolled Agent, I've spent years helping business owners legally reduce taxes.

One thing I've learned is that the IRS doesn't dislike creative tax planning.

The IRS dislikes bad documentation.

That's an important difference.

Every year I meet business owners who miss thousands of dollars in perfectly legitimate deductions.

I also meet people who try to deduct their family pet because it "keeps them company while they work."

Nice try.

The IRS has heard that one before.

But here's where things get interesting.

Some animals really do have jobs.

Not pretend jobs.

Real jobs.

Some protect equipment worth hundreds of thousands of dollars.

Some appear in advertising campaigns.

Some attract customers.

Some calm anxious clients.

Some herd livestock.

Some generate millions of social media views.

Those animals aren't simply pets.

They're business assets.

And business assets can create legitimate deductions when the facts support them.

That's what this book is about.

Not loopholes.

Not tricks.

Not stretching the truth.

Just understanding the rules better than most people do.

Throughout these pages, we'll meet remarkable working animals.

You'll discover how a bakery cat increased sales.

Why one German Shepherd was worth more than a security system.

How one Golden Retriever accidentally became a marketing celebrity.

And why one business owner nearly lost thousands because they skipped one simple piece of paperwork.

You'll laugh.

You'll probably look at your own pet a little differently.

Most importantly...

You'll learn how to separate wishful thinking from legitimate tax planning.

By the end of this book, you'll know exactly where the IRS draws the line—and how to stay safely on the right side of it.

So grab your favorite drink.

Scratch your dog's ears.

Tell your cat she's temporarily in charge.

Let's find out if your favorite employee has four legs.

EVERY RECEIPT
TELLS A STORY.
EVERY NAP
RESTORES POWER.
Naps
Improve
Numbers
CAT TAX
CODE
PURR-SONAL
DEDUCTIONS
CAT
TO DO:
NAP
EAT
PLAY
NAP AGAIN
REPEAT
PET SUPPLIES
TOTAL $23.87
VETERINARY
CLINIC
TOTAL $126.00
PETSMART
Toy Mouse
Kitty Condo
Treats
TOTAL $34.61
TOTAL $27.98
THANK YOU!

Part I

Can Pets Really Save You Money?

Chapter 1

So...Can My Dog Really Be a Tax Deduction?

I get this question almost every week.

Sometimes people whisper it.

Sometimes they laugh before they ask.

Sometimes they look around first to make sure nobody else heard them. Then they say: "This might sound crazy..."

I smile.

Because I already know what's coming.

"My dog..."

"...can I deduct him?"

The answer surprises almost everyone.

Sometimes.

Not always.

That's probably not the answer you were hoping for.

But it's the honest one.

Meet Charlie

Charlie is a beautiful Golden Retriever.

Every morning at exactly 8:15, Charlie arrives at a real estate office.

He greets clients.

Children adore him.

Nervous buyers relax the moment they pet him.

He appears in nearly every Facebook post.

He's featured on the company's website.

He's even been on billboards.

One day his owner asked me,

"So...is Charlie deductible?"

My answer wasn't about Charlie.

It was about Charlie's job.

The IRS doesn't ask,

"Is Charlie adorable?"

(He is.)

The IRS asks,

"Why is Charlie part of this business?" That's the question that matters.

Pets vs. Employees

Imagine two dogs.

The first spends all day sleeping on the couch.

The second patrols a fenced construction yard every night.

Both eat the same dog food.

Both visit the same veterinarian.

Both chase squirrels.

Only one is helping produce business income.

That's where taxes begin.

The IRS doesn't tax cuteness.

It recognizes business purpose.

That's an important distinction.

The Belly Rub Test

Here's my favorite way to explain it.

Imagine your pet disappeared tomorrow.

Would your business notice?

If the answer is:

"Not really..."

Then your pet is probably just a beloved companion.

If the answer is:

"Customers would ask where he went." "Our security would be worse."

"Our marketing wouldn't be the same." "We'd lose an important part of the business."

Now we're having a completely different conversation.

Paw Print Tip

Don't ask: "Can I deduct my pet?"

Instead ask:

"What job does my pet perform for my business?"

One question creates arguments.

The other creates documentation.

Myth vs. Fact

Myth

Every business owner can deduct their dog. False.

Fact

Some business owners may deduct certain expenses for animals that perform legitimate business functions and are properly documented.

That's less exciting.

But it's much more accurate.

The IRS Isn't Anti-Dog

People often imagine IRS auditors sitting around looking for reasons to reject pet deductions.

That's not how it works.

An auditor wants evidence.

If you tell them your German Shepherd guards your equipment yard...

Show them.

If you say your Border Collie appears in advertising...

Show them.

If your bakery cat attracts customers...

Show them.

Evidence wins.

Stories alone don't.

Tail-Wagging Tax Tip

The best deductions are never surprises.

They're documented all year long.

Take photos.

Save receipts.

Keep notes.

Treat your working animal the same way you'd document any other business asset.

Future-you will be grateful.

Chapter 2

Why the IRS Says "Usually No"

"The IRS doesn't have a problem with your dog. They have a problem with people trying to deduct their family pet without a business reason."

The Most Expensive Belly Rub You'll Ever Give

Every tax season, someone walks into my office and says something like:

"My neighbor deducts his dog, so I figured I could too."

That sentence has probably cost taxpayers more money than almost any other pet-related myth.

Tax law isn't based on what your neighbor did, what someone posted on social media, or what your cousin's barber claimed happened during an audit. It's based on the facts of your situation.

Most pets are personal companions. That means the cost of feeding them, grooming them, boarding them, and taking them to the veterinarian is generally considered a personal expense— not a business deduction.

That answer disappoints some people.

It also protects them.

Imagine if the IRS allowed everyone to deduct every pet. Overnight, millions of Labradors, Siamese cats, guinea pigs, and parakeets would magically become "business assets." That's not how the tax system works.

The IRS starts with a simple assumption:

Pets are personal unless you can demonstrate otherwise. That doesn't mean the answer is always "no." It means you need a better question.

The Umbrella Story

Picture yourself standing outside on a sunny day carrying an umbrella.

People will assume it's for the weather.

Now imagine it's not raining.

Suddenly everyone wants to know why you're carrying it.

Your pet deduction works the same way.

The IRS assumes your dog is your pet.

If you're claiming business expenses, you need to explain why this situation is different.

When there's a legitimate business purpose and solid documentation, that explanation can be straightforward.

A Tale of Two Dogs

Let's meet two nearly identical Golden Retrievers.

Daisy

Daisy lives with the Thompson family.

She enjoys belly rubs, long walks, and stealing socks from the laundry basket.

She has never met a stranger.

She has no business responsibilities.

Her expenses are personal.

That's perfectly normal.

Ranger

Ranger also enjoys belly rubs.

But every evening he patrols a fenced storage yard owned by an electrical contractor.

Security cameras frequently capture him making rounds.

Customers know him.

Employees depend on him.

His trainer provides annual certifications.

His veterinarian keeps records showing he remains fit for working duties.

Same species.

Same breed.

Different facts.

The IRS isn't treating dogs differently because one is more lovable.

It treats them differently because one has a documented business function.

Pet Tax Tip

Never try to make your pet fit a deduction.

Instead, determine whether the facts already support one.

Good tax planning starts with reality—not wishful thinking.

What About Working from Home?

This is where people get into trouble.

Working from home doesn't automatically transform your pet into a business expense.

If your dog lies next to your desk while you answer emails, that's companionship.

If your dog patrols your detached workshop after hours because expensive equipment is stored there, that's a different analysis.

The details matter.

Myth vs. Fact

Myth

"My dog is always with me while I work."

Fact

Being present isn't the same as performing a business function.

Myth

"I put my company logo on my dog's bandana."

Fact

A logo alone doesn't create a deduction.

The animal still needs a genuine business role.

Myth

"The IRS never checks these things."

Fact

The IRS examines documentation—not assumptions.

The Three Questions I Ask Every Client

Whenever someone asks whether their pet could qualify, I begin with three questions.

What does the animal do?

Not what could it do.

Not what you'd like it to do.

What is it going to do today?

Would the business operate differently without the animal?

If nothing changes...you probably don't have a business expense.

If customers notice...

Security changes...

Marketing suffers...

Now we have something worth exploring.

Can you prove it?

Photos.

Receipts.

Training records.

Social media posts.

Customer comments.

Security logs.

Evidence beats opinions every time.

Barking Up the Right Tree

The biggest mistake I see isn't aggressive tax planning.

It's lazy documentation.

Business owners often have perfectly legitimate situations but fail to record them.

Then, years later, they try to remember details after receiving an IRS letter.

That's backward.

Documentation should happen while the business activity is taking place.

Your future self will thank you.

Chapter Checklist

Understand that most pets are personal.

Know that some working animals may qualify.

Focus on facts instead of assumptions.

Start documenting today, not after-tax season.

ELITE
TAX & FINANCIAL
SOLUTIONS
Your Success. Our Strategy
STRONG
FAMILIES
STRONG
BUSINESSES
CEO
FAMILY.
INTEGRITY.
TAX SMART.
FUTURE READY.
CFO
TEAMWORK
TRUST
TAX STRATEGY
SUCCESS
TAX PLANNING
BUSINESS STRATEGY
WEALTH BUILDING
Plan Today
Save Tomorrow
Build Legacy

Chapter 3

When Pets Become Business Assets

"Some employees ask for bonuses. Others ask for tennis balls."

One afternoon I met with a landscape contractor named Ben.

As we reviewed his business expenses, I noticed several photographs on his office wall.

Every single picture featured the same black Labrador.

The dog was standing beside trailers.

Watching over equipment.

Riding in the company truck.

Greeting customers.

Finally, I asked,

"Tell me about your employee."

Ben laughed.

"That's not an employee."

"That's Duke."

I smiled.

"I think Duke may have been working longer than some of your staff."

Ben had never considered that possibility.

To him, Duke was simply family.

But businesses often have assets that are also beloved companions.

The question isn't whether you love your pet.

The question is whether your pet performs a genuine business role.

What Is a Business Asset?

When people hear the phrase business asset, they usually picture:

Computers

Trucks

Buildings

Machinery

Office furniture

Animals rarely make the list.

Yet throughout history, businesses have relied on animals.

Ranches depend on livestock guardian dogs.

Mounted patrol companies rely on horses.

Police departments use K-9 officers.

Search-and-rescue organizations train dogs for years before they ever begin working.

Animals have always been business assets.

The tax treatment depends on the facts.

More Than Mascots

Some animals earn their keep in less obvious ways.

A bookstore's resident cat becomes a local attraction.

A vineyard's Border Collie appears in every advertisement.

A real estate team's Golden Retriever stars in listing videos viewed hundreds of thousands of times.

These animals aren't just decorations.

They're part of the brand.

When a business intentionally uses an animal to attract customers or generate revenue, it's worth evaluating the related expenses under the applicable tax rules.

Meet Olive

Olive is a mixed-breed rescue dog.

She spends every Saturday greeting customers at a family-owned garden center.

Children ask for her by name.

Customers photograph her beside seasonal displays.

The store even created an annual "Photos with Olive" event that benefits the local animal shelter.

The event increases foot traffic.

It generates publicity.

It supports the community.

And it strengthens the business's brand.

Olive isn't merely present.

She contributes to customer experience.

That's a meaningful distinction.

Pet Tax Tip

Ask yourself: "If I hired a person to perform this same function, would I consider their compensation a business expense?"

While animals aren't employees in the legal sense, the question helps identify whether a real

business purpose exists.

Looking Ahead

In the next chapter, we'll meet the hardest-working dogs in business:

The guard dogs.

Some protect warehouses.

Some patrol construction yards.

Some watch over farms.

And some may save their owners more money than the latest security system ever could.

PART II
THE WORKING PETS

Chapter 4

Guard Dogs That Earn Their Kibble

"Some security systems come with monthly monitoring. Others come with muddy paw prints."

Meet Hank

Every evening at 6:00 p.m., Hank clocks in.

No timecard.

No employee badge.

No coffee break.

Just a slow walk around a fencing contractor's equipment yard.

Hank is a 95-pound German Shepherd who knows every gate, every truck, and every unusual sound.

One night someone climbed the back fence.

They didn't stay long.

The security camera captured Hank running toward the intruder.

The next frame showed someone climbing back over the fence much faster than they came in.

The owner laughed when he showed me the footage.

"Best investment I've ever made."

He wasn't talking about the fence.

He was talking about Hank.

Dogs Have Protected Businesses for Centuries

Before there were alarm systems...there were dogs.

Long before motion detectors, infrared cameras, and smartphone alerts, businesses relied on animals to protect valuable property.

Farmers.

Warehouse owners.

Construction companies.

Storage facilities.

Equipment yards.

Guard dogs aren't a new idea.

The tax question isn't whether dogs can provide security.

It's whether the expenses connected to a working guard dog qualify under the tax rules based on the specific facts and circumstances.

Security Isn't Cute...

It's Business

Imagine owning a plumbing company.

Inside your fenced yard sits:

- $300,000 worth of trucks

- $150,000 worth of tools
- Copper pipe
- Generators
- Compressors
- Heavy equipment

Would you buy security cameras?

Probably.

Would you install fencing?

Probably.

Would you hire security?

Maybe.

If a properly trained guard dog genuinely serves that security function, it may be appropriate to evaluate related costs under the same general business-expense principles that apply to other ordinary and necessary security measures.

The key is the business purpose—and the documentation.

The Difference Between Buddy and Bullet

Let's compare two dogs.

Buddy

Buddy sleeps in the house.

He loves peanut butter.

He barks at squirrels.

He occasionally scares the mail carrier.

Buddy is wonderful.

Buddy is also a family pet.

Bullet

Bullet sleeps in a kennel beside an industrial warehouse.

He patrols every evening.

He receives professional protection training.

Employees know his schedule.

Customers know not to enter after hours.

Security logs mention him.

The insurance company knows he's there.

Different facts.

Different analysis.

Pet Tax Tip

If your guard dog has a business role, document it throughout the year.

Don't wait until tax season to remember what happened.

Real Security Means Real Records

One of the biggest mistakes business owners make is assuming everyone already knows what the dog does.

The IRS doesn't.

An auditor wasn't there at midnight when your dog scared away trespassers.

That's why documentation matters.

Good records might include:

- Training certificates
- Veterinary records
- Photos of the dog on duty
- Security policies
- Incident logs
- Insurance documents
- Business photographs
- Employee statements

The goal isn't to overwhelm anyone with paperwork.

The goal is to show that the dog's role in the business is genuine and well documented.

The Belly Rub Rule

Here's something I tell clients.

A guard dog can absolutely enjoy life.

Playing fetch doesn't cancel out legitimate work.

Sleeping on the porch doesn't automatically make every expense deductible.

Many business assets have personal aspects.

The important question is whether the animal actually performs a business function and how those facts are documented.

Myth vs. Fact

Myth

Only police dogs can qualify.

Fact

Businesses may use working dogs for many legitimate purposes, depending on the facts.

Myth

Big dogs automatically qualify.

Fact

Size doesn't determine tax treatment.

Business purpose does.

Myth

Putting up a "Beware of Dog" sign creates a deduction.

Fact

Signs don't create business use.

Facts do.

IRS Watch-Out

If the dog spends nearly all its time inside the family home and only occasionally wanders outside, claiming that it provides full-time commercial security may be difficult to support.

Be honest.

Good tax planning never requires exaggeration.

Tail-Wagging Tax Tip

Your documentation should tell a story.

If someone who had never met your dog could understand its role in your business after reviewing your records, you're moving in the right direction.

Chapter 5

Shop Cats That Bring Customers

"Sometimes the best salesperson in the store takes naps between customers."

Walk into enough small businesses, and you'll eventually meet the unofficial manager.

Sometimes it's behind the cash register.

Sometimes it's sleeping in the front window.

Sometimes it ignores everyone.

Because...It's a cat.

Meet Oliver

Oliver lives in a small independent bookstore.

Customers come in asking for him by name.

Children search every aisle trying to find where he's sleeping today.

People take selfies.

They post them online.

They tag the bookstore.

Some customers buy books.

Others buy coffee.

Many come back simply because Oliver works there.

Does Oliver know he's helping the business?

Probably not.

Cats aren't known for caring about quarterly sales goals.

But the owner certainly notices.

The Marketing Cat

Years ago, businesses bought billboards.

Today...

Many businesses build relationships.

People love stories.

People love animals.

Put the two together and remarkable things happen.

A bakery posts a photo of its sleepy cat.

Ten thousand people see it.

A winery shares videos of its vineyard dog.

Customers plan weekend visits.

A hardware store's parrot learns to say,

"Need any screws?"

Suddenly the bird becomes a local celebrity.

The point isn't that animals are magical.

The point is that some businesses intentionally use animals as part of their customer experience and marketing.

When that role is real and documented, it deserves careful evaluation under the applicable tax rules.

More Than Entertainment

A shop cat may help:

- Create a memorable customer experience
- Increase repeat visits
- Generate social media engagement
- Build community recognition
- Strengthen the business brand

Those aren't guarantees of a deduction.

They're examples of business functions that may be relevant depending on the facts.

Customer Test

Here's a question I love asking.

"If your customers walked in tomorrow and the animal wasn't there, would anyone ask about it?"

If the answer is yes...

That's interesting.

When customers mention the animal in online reviews, photos, testimonials, or conversations, it suggests the animal is part of the customer experience—not just a pet that happens to be nearby.

Pet Tax Tip

Save screenshots.

Social media posts disappear.

Customer comments are getting buried.

If your business animal appears in marketing or customer interactions, keep records showing how it's being used.

Myth vs. Fact

Myth

Every shop cat is deductible.

Fact

No. Each situation depends on how the animal is used, how expenses relate to the business, and whether the role is supported by documentation.

Chapter 6

Social Media Pets That Pay Their Own Way

"Some influencers wear designer clothes. Others shed on them."

Not long ago, a client showed me her company's Instagram account.

Every third photo featured her French Bulldog, Winston.

Winston wasn't an accident.

He had become the face of the brand.

Customers expected to see him.

They commented about him.

They shared his videos.

They even bought merchandise with his picture.

The business owner laughed.

"I think people like Winston more than they like me." That happens more often than you might think.

The Modern Business Mascot

Marketing has changed dramatically.

People don't always connect with logos.

They connect with stories.

Animals create emotional connections.

A dog greeting customers in a video.

A ranch horse featured in advertisements.

A winery's Border Collie running through vineyards.

These images help businesses stand out.

When an animal genuinely becomes part of a company's marketing strategy, it's worth discussing with your tax professional how related expenses should be analyzed and documented.

Not Every Viral Video Creates a Deduction

Here's the important part.

One funny TikTok doesn't suddenly transform your pet into a business asset.

The business use needs to be intentional, recurring, and connected to the company's activities.

That's why keeping records matters just as much here as it does for any other business expense.

Marketing with Purpose

If your pet is part of your brand, consider keeping:

Content calendars

Advertising invoices

Photo shoot receipts

Social media analytics

Marketing plans

Campaign results

These records help explain how the animal fits into your overall marketing efforts.

Pet Tax Tip

Think like a marketing director.

Would you keep records for a paid advertising campaign?

If your pet is part of that campaign, keep records for that too.

Chapter 7

Farm Animals That Earn Their Hay

"On a farm, every animal has a job. The trick is knowing which jobs matter for tax purposes."

Meet Molly

Molly isn't glamorous.

She doesn't have an Instagram account.

She isn't wearing a designer collar.

She has never been featured in a television commercial.

Instead...

Molly spends every night walking the fence line.

She's a Great Pyrenees.

Her office is 160 acres.

Her coworkers are 400 sheep.

Her biggest challenge?

Coyotes.

If you've never owned livestock, you might think Molly is just another big white dog.

The rancher knows better.

Without Molly, lamb losses would increase.

Veterinary costs would climb.

Insurance claims might rise.

Predators don't care about business hours.

Fortunately...

Neither does Molly.

Every Employee Doesn't Wear a Tie

Business owners sometimes picture "business assets" as trucks, tractors, or expensive machinery.

Farmers often smile when I say that.

They know something many city businesses don't.

Sometimes the most valuable asset has four legs.

Herding dogs.

Livestock guardian dogs.

Working horses.

Even certain pest-control animals.

They aren't simply present on the property.

They're part of daily operations.

Meet Tex

Tex is a Border Collie.

Every morning before sunrise, he begins work.

He moves cattle.

Separates calves.

Guides livestock through gates.

Helps reduce stress on the herd.

If you've ever watched a skilled stock dog work, it's hard not to be impressed.

Tex doesn't replace employees.

He makes everyone else more efficient.

That's real economic value.

Business Purpose Matters

Whether it's a livestock guardian, herding dog, or another working animal, the tax analysis isn't based on affection.

It's based on function.

Questions might include:

- What job does the animal perform?
- How often is that work performed?
- Is it ordinary for this type of business?
- How is the role documented?
- Which expenses relate to that business use?

Those questions are much more important than the animal's breed or personality.

Pet Tax Tip

Working animals deserve working records.

Keep:

- Veterinary invoices
- Training records
- Breeding records (when applicable)

- Photographs
- Purchase documents
- Employment or ranch logs
- Security reports
- Livestock records

Good records tell the story long before anyone asks.

The Goat That Saved the Day

One client owned several acres surrounding a commercial property.

Instead of paying a landscaping company thousands of dollars every year, they hired a goat grazing business to clear invasive brush.

The goats weren't the client's animals, but the story illustrates an important point:

Animals perform valuable business services every day.

Sometimes they're contractors.

Sometimes they're business assets.

Sometimes they're simply part of how work gets done.

Myth vs. Fact

Myth

Farm animals automatically qualify as business expenses.

Fact

Not automatically.

Their role, the business context, and the applicable tax rules determine how expenses are treated.

Myth

Only dogs can qualify.

Fact

Different kinds of animals may serve legitimate business functions in different industries.

The analysis depends on the facts.

Barnyard Wisdom

Farmers rarely ask,

"Can I deduct my dog?"

Instead, they ask,

"How do I properly account for my working animals?" That's exactly the right question.

Chapter 8

Therapy Animals, Service Animals & Office Pets

"Sometimes the hardest-working employee is the one making everyone smile."

Walk into some counseling offices, and you'll find soft music.

Comfortable chairs.

Warm lighting.

And...

A Golden Retriever quietly sleeping beside the couch.

Coincidence?

Not usually.

Meet Rosie

Rosie works in a counseling practice.

Children arrive nervous.

Some are frightened.

Some refuse to speak.

Rosie never asks questions.

She simply walks over...

Lies down...

And waits.

Many young clients begin talking while petting her.

Parents often mention Rosie in thank-you notes.

The therapist didn't buy Rosie as a tax strategy.

She became part of the practice because she genuinely helped clients.

Understanding the Difference

People often use terms like:

- Therapy dog
- Emotional support animal
- Service animal

... interchangeably.

From a legal and tax perspective, they are not necessarily the same thing.

Each has different rules, and those rules can affect how expenses are analyzed.

That's one reason it's important to avoid assumptions and evaluate each situation individually.

Office Dogs

Office dogs have become increasingly common.

Some businesses find they:

- Improve morale

- Make customers feel welcome
- Create memorable experiences
- Encourages conversation

That's wonderful.

But remember...

Simply allowing a pet to come to work doesn't automatically create a business deduction.

The role still needs to be supported by the facts.

Pet Tax Tip

If your animal has a genuine role in your business, document that role.

Photos, policies, schedules, customer feedback, and written descriptions can all help explain how the animal fits into your operations.

The Coffee Shop Dog

One of my favorite stories involves a neighborhood coffee shop.

Their Labrador greeted nearly every customer.

Children looked forward to seeing him.

Regulars asked where he was if he stayed home.

Eventually, the business began featuring him in newsletters, holiday promotions, and community events.

Did that automatically answer every tax question?

No.

But it certainly demonstrated that the dog had become part of the customer experience rather than simply being someone's personal pet.

IRS Watch-Out

When an animal serves both personal and business purposes, careful allocation and documentation become especially important.

Mixed-use situations often require more thoughtful analysis than all-business or all-personal situations.

Chapter 9

The Paperwork That Protects Everything

"Receipts may not be exciting—but they can be worth thousands of dollars."

Here's a secret.

The best tax strategy in the world...

Can fail because of bad paperwork.

I've seen perfectly reasonable deductions denied simply because the records didn't tell the story.

I've also seen challenging situations succeed because the documentation was organized, consistent, and credible.

Think Like a Storyteller

Imagine handing your records to someone who has never visited your business.

Would they understand:

- What does your animal do?
- Why does the role matter?
- How often does it perform that role?
- Which expenses relate to that work?

If the answer is yes...

You're making life easier for everyone.

The Pet Business Binder

I recommend creating a single folder—digital or paper—for your working animal.

Include things like:

Purchase or adoption records

Veterinary invoices

Training certificates

Photographs

Marketing materials

Business policies

Insurance documents Receipts

Social media screenshots

Written descriptions of the animal's business role. Think of it as your pet's business résumé.

One Picture Really Can Help

Suppose you claim your German Shepherd patrols your equipment yard.

Now imagine you also have:

- Photos of the dog at the yard
- Security camera stills
- Employee statements
- A written security policy
- Annual training records

That's a much stronger story than saying,

"Trust me."

Pet Tax Tip

Don't document because you're afraid of an audit.

Document because good businesses keep good records.

Audits are simply one reason those records matter.

Myth vs. Fact

Myth

"I'll remember everything next April."

Fact

Most people won't.

Write it down while it's fresh.

Myth

"Receipts are enough."

Fact

Receipts show that you spent money.

They don't necessarily explain why the expense relates to your business.

Coming Next

In the next section, we'll cover:

- Common mistakes business owners make
- What happens if the IRS asks questions

- How to organize your records before anyone ever requests them
- Real-world examples of good—and bad—documentation

PART III
MAKING IT LEGAL

Chapter 10

The Biggest Mistakes Business Owners Make

"The IRS doesn't expect perfection. It expects honesty."

Every tax season I see the same five mistakes.

Not because people are dishonest.

Because they've heard advice from:

- Facebook
- TikTok
- Their brother-in-law
- Their barber
- "A guy I know..."

None of those people are signing your tax return.

Let's fix that.

Mistake #1

"Everybody Does It."

This may be the most expensive sentence in America.

"My neighbor deducts his dog."

"My cousin deducts his horse." "My friend writes off his aquarium."

Wonderful.

None of those facts determine whether you have a deductible expense.

Every deduction stands on its own facts.

Mistake #2

No Documentation

Imagine walking into an IRS examination.

The examiner asks,

"So tell me about your guard dog."

You answer...

"Well...

... everyone knows he's a guard dog."

Unfortunately...

The IRS doesn't know him.

Documentation introduces your dog long before you do.

Mistake #3

Trying Too Hard

Some business owners become so excited about the possibility of deductions that suddenly...

Every pet becomes an employee.

Your Chihuahua isn't Head of Human Resources.

Your cat isn't Director of Operations.

Your hamster isn't Vice President of Marketing.

Humor is great.

Tax returns aren't the place for it.

Mistake #4

Forgetting Personal Use

Many legitimate working animals are also beloved family pets.

That's perfectly normal.

But pretending personal use doesn't exist usually weakens your position rather than strengthening it.

Honest allocation often creates a much stronger story.

Mistake #5

Waiting Until Tax Time

Tax planning doesn't happen in April.

It happens in January.

And February.

And March.

By the time April arrives...

You're mostly organizing what already happened.

Pet Tax Tip

Good tax planning feels boring while you're doing it.

Great documentation almost always does.

Then one day...

You realize those boring records saved thousands of dollars.

Chapter 11

Could Your Pet Survive an IRS Audit?

"Audits don't begin with panic. They begin with paperwork."

Nobody likes getting letters from the IRS.

Even tax professionals.

Trust me.

When that envelope arrives...

Nobody says,

"Oh good!

Something exciting!"

Fortunately...

Most audits aren't dramatic.

They're conversations supported by documents.

Meet Susan

Susan owned a small wedding venue.

Her Great Pyrenees, Belle, protected the property overnight.

Belle was featured on the venue website.

Guests loved taking pictures with her.

When the IRS requested additional documentation, Susan didn't panic.

She opened a folder.

Inside were:

- Training records
- Veterinary invoices
- Photos
- Security policies
- Insurance information
- Website screenshots
- Social media posts
- Maintenance logs

The conversation became much easier.

Not because Belle was adorable.

Because Belle's role was documented.

What Auditors Usually Want

They aren't looking for tricks.

They're looking for answers.

Questions like:

What business purpose does the animal serve?

How often?

Where?

What records support that claim?

How were expenses determined?

If your records answer those questions clearly...

You're already ahead of many taxpayers.

Think Like a Journalist

Pretend someone from your local newspaper visits your business.

Could they write an article explaining exactly what your animal does?

If yes...

Your documentation is probably moving in the right direction.

IRS Watch-Out

Never create documents after receiving an audit notice and pretend they existed beforehand.

Auditors have seen that before.

Honesty is always the better strategy.

Pet Tax Tip

Good documentation protects more than deductions.

It protects your credibility.

And credibility matters.

Chapter 12

The Pet Business Playbook

"Every successful business follows systems. Your documentation should too."

Here's something I've learned after years as an Enrolled Agent.

Successful businesses rarely depend on memory.

They depend on systems.

Let's build one.

Step One

Create a folder called: Working

Animal Records

That's it.

Simple.

Inside, create folders for:

- Veterinary
- Training
- Marketing
- Security
- Photos
- Receipts
- Insurance
- Notes

Step Two

Every month...Take five minutes.

Ask yourself:

Did my pet perform business activities this month?

If yes...Add evidence. One picture. One receipt. One note.

Repeat twelve times.

Congratulations.

You now have a year's worth of documentation.

Step Three

Review everything before tax season.

Not after.

This is when you'll notice:

- Missing receipts.
- Missing photographs.
- Missing explanations.

Much easier to fix in February than two years later.

The Smartphone Strategy

You already carry the best documentation tool ever invented.

Your phone.

Use it.

Snap pictures.

Record short videos.

Save screenshots.

Email yourself notes.

Technology makes recordkeeping easier than ever.

The Annual Pet Review

Every January, ask:

Has my pet's business role changed?

Has marketing increased?

Security changed?

New training?

New responsibilities?

Your documentation should grow with your business.

Pet Tax Tip

Don't document because you expect an audit.

Document because professionals document.

That's simply how successful businesses operate.

PART IV
STORIES FROM AN ENROLLED AGENT

Chapter 13

The Dog That Sold More Houses

Every town has one.

The real estate office with the famous dog.

In this case...His name was Murphy.

Murphy appeared in nearly every listing video.

Children loved him.

Buyers remembered him.

Sellers specifically asked if Murphy would appear during open houses. One day I asked the Realtor, "How many people mention Murphy?"

She laughed.

"Almost everybody."

Murphy wasn't closing transactions.

He wasn't negotiating contracts.

But he had become an important part of the company's brand.

That matters.

Because businesses spend thousands of dollars every year trying to become memorable.

Murphy already was.

Chapter 14

The Cat That Outsold the Advertising Budget

An antique store adopted a stray cat.

Nothing fancy.

Just a friendly orange cat.

Visitors started taking photos.

Then posting them online.

Then bringing friends.

Soon...

People visited just to see the cat.

Did they leave empty-handed? Usually not. One customer joked,

"I came for the cat...

... and accidentally bought a $900 dining table."

Marketing sometimes arrives in unexpected packages.

Chapter 15

The Dog That Almost Cost Everything

Not every story ends happily.

A contractor claimed nearly every expense for his Labrador.

Food.

Beds.

Toys.

Vacation boarding.

No records.

No explanation.

Just receipts.

When questioned...He couldn't explain what the dog actually did.

The deduction disappeared.

The penalties didn't.

The lesson wasn't:

Don't deduct working animals.

The lesson was:

Don't confuse family expenses with legitimate business expenses.

Documentation matters. Facts matter. Truth matters.

PART V
Putting It All Together

NO
PROB-LLAMA
WE SOLVE
PROBLEMS
STAY
FOCUSED
AND
KEEP
BALANCING
INVOICE
INVOICES
INVOICES
INVOICES
INVOICES
INVOICES
I ♥
SPREADSHEETS
LLAMA, CPA
ACCOUNTS
RECEIVABLE

Chapter 16

Could Your Pet Qualify?

"This chapter won't give you permission to deduct your pet. It will help you ask better questions."

After reading this book, you may be looking at your four-legged companion a little differently.

That's okay.

The goal isn't to convince yourself your pet is deductible.

The goal is to understand when further analysis is worthwhile.

So let's walk through a practical checklist.

The Five-Question Test

Question 1

Does your pet perform a genuine business function?

Examples might include:

Protecting business property

Herding livestock

Serving in a documented therapeutic role within a business

Appearing as part of an intentional marketing strategy

Performing another identifiable business task

If the answer is "not really," you're probably done.

If the answer is "yes," continue.

Question 2

Would the business operate differently without the animal?

If customers notice...

If security changes...

If operations become more difficult...

The answer may be yes.

Question 3

Can you explain the role in one sentence?

For example:

"Our German Shepherd patrols our fenced commercial equipment yard after business hours."

Or:

"Our Border Collie appears in our paid marketing campaigns and company branding."

Simple.

Clear.

Honest.

Question 4

Can you support your explanation?

Think about:

✓ Photos

✓ Videos

✓ Receipts

✓ Marketing materials

✓ Training records

✓ Written policies

✓ Insurance documents

Question 5

Would you be comfortable explaining everything to an IRS examiner?

If your answer is yes...

You're approaching the issue the right way.

The Paw Print Scorecard

Give yourself one point for each "yes."

Question	Yes
Business purpose	x
Business changes without pet	x
Easy explanation	x
Documentation	x
Comfortable explaining it	x

5 Points

Excellent.

Now talk with your Enrolled Agent or tax professional.

3–4 Points Interesting.

More documentation or clarification may be needed.

0–2 Points

Your pet is probably exactly what he or she should be:

A wonderful companion.

Frequently Asked Questions

Can I deduct my puppy?

Only if the puppy has a legitimate business role and the applicable tax rules support the expense.

Being adorable isn't enough.

(Unfortunately.)

My dog appears in Facebook posts.

Does that qualify?

Maybe.

The important questions are:

- Is the use intentional?
- Is it part of your business marketing?
- Can you document it?
- How do the related expenses connect to that business use?

My cat sleeps in my office.

Does that count?

Usually not by itself.

Many pets enjoy office naps.

That's companionship.

Business use requires more than simply being present.

Can horses qualify?

Sometimes.

Working horses used in farming, ranching, breeding, or other businesses may raise different tax considerations than recreational horses.

The facts matter.

What about emotional support animals?

The tax treatment depends on the specific circumstances and the applicable rules.

Don't assume the answer based solely on the label.

Should I ask my tax preparer?

Absolutely.

In fact..If your preparer immediately says,

"Pets are never deductible," or "Everything is deductible," consider asking a few more questions.

The right answer is usually:

"Tell me about your situation."

The Ten Golden Rules

1. Don't invent business use.
2. Document everything.
3. Keep receipts.
4. Take photographs.
5. Save marketing materials.
6. Separate business and personal expenses whenever possible.
7. Review documentation annually.
8. Be honest.
9. Stay organized.
10. When in doubt...

Ask a qualified Enrolled Agent.

Final Thoughts

Sometimes the Best Employee Has Four Legs

When I first became an Enrolled Agent, I never imagined I'd spend part of my career talking about dogs, cats, horses, goats, and even the occasional llama.

Yet here we are.

This book was never about finding clever loopholes.

It was about looking more carefully.

Sometimes business owners miss opportunities because they're afraid to ask questions.

Other times they create problems because they stop asking questions too soon.

Good tax planning lives somewhere in the middle.

If this book has taught you anything, I hope it's this:

The IRS doesn't reward creativity.

It rewards accuracy.

A well-documented business purpose is far more valuable than a clever story.

Whether your business includes a guard dog protecting expensive equipment, a vineyard dog greeting visitors, a shop cat charming customers, or a ranch horse helping manage livestock, your responsibility is the same:

- Know the facts.
- Keep good records.
- Seek professional advice.

And remember...Your favorite employee may have four legs.

But your best business decision will always be keeping honest records and following the law.

Thank you for reading.

I hope you and your furry coworkers have many successful—and well-documented—years ahead.

About the Author

Cathi Korelin, Enrolled Agent

Cathi Korelin is an Enrolled Agent, Tax Strategist, and founder of Elite Tax Inc. & Family Office. She works with business owners, real estate investors, professionals, and families to develop proactive tax strategies, bookkeeping systems, probate accounting solutions, and family office services.

Known for translating complex tax concepts into practical guidance, Cathi enjoys helping clients understand opportunities they may not have considered while emphasizing accurate documentation and long-term planning.

When she's not helping clients navigate tax law, she's educating business owners through speaking, writing, and practical resources designed to make taxes easier to understand.

For more information:

Elite Tax Inc. & Family Office

cathi@elitetaxinc.com

www.ingramcontent.com/pod-product-compliance
Lightning Source LLC
LaVergne TN
LVHW051941051126
851857LV00001B/6

* 9 7 9 8 2 5 6 2 8 9 9 0 4 *